TRISH'S TREASURES IN RHYME

Trish Bishop

ISBN: 9798648419605

CONTENTS

FOREWARD

Trish Bishop is a gifted writer who composes in true biblical fashion under the inspiration of the Holy Spirit.

Her collection of teaching poetry is totally unique and makes for compelling reading.

It is eminently suitable for both children and Christian disciples who, according to Jesus, are the 'little ones' who will inherit and then inhabit the future coming and eternal Kingdom of God. Read and enjoy!

Stan Noonan BA (Hons.)

ACKNOWLEDGEMENTS

Many thanks to dear friends who encouraged me to write this book.

Thanks to dear Pam and Dave Nickson for editing and helping me to publish it.

I do pray that many readers will be truly blessed and encouraged as they read this book for themselves.

God bless,

Trish Bishop

LET ME INTRODUCE YOU TO MY JESUS...

Who took my place and died upon the cross,
He rose again and sat right down in heaven,
He sure showed the devil who is boss.
I would like you to meet Him,
For He wants to show you that He cares,
I know He is the only way to the Father,
I guess you could say He is the stairs.
So come now let me introduce you,
A sinner you won't always be,
Jesus died for you 'cos He loves you,
And wants you in His family.

Trish Bishop.

RHYMES FROM
SCRIPTURE

IN THE BEGINNING

In the beginning God said,
"Let there be light,
The sun for the day,
The moon for the night."

Then God divided the waters,
And the earth did appear,
That He had a plan,
Became very clear.

Then God made the seeds,
For all kinds of food,
Told them to be fruitful,
And God saw it was good.

He turned to the waters and said,
"Let there be,
All kinds of living creatures,
To live in the sea."

Then God made the creatures,
To walk and creep on the earth,
Told them to multiply,
With all of their worth.

Then God made the birds,
The heavens to share,
With all kinds of insects,
That fly in the air.

Then God made man in His image,
And instructed him to be,
The ruler and carer of all creatures,
On the land and in the sea.

On the last day God saw all was good,
And with love He blessed it,
God finished His work and,
On this day He rested.

Taken from Genesis 1

IN THE GARDEN OF EDEN

God breathed life into His man,
After He had formed him from the dust.
Now he was a living being,
In whom God could put His trust.

For He placed him in the Garden of Eden,
Saying, *"Tend it well for me,*
Of every tree there you may eat,
Except the good and evil knowledge tree."

This tree, God had put in the garden to test His man,
For He wanted him to be loyal,
And to do the best he can.

Then God saw that it was not good,
For Adam to be all alone,
So God made all the cattle,
And other beasts for Adam to own.

But although Adam named them all,
He found not one to keep,
God said, *"A helpmeet I will make for him."*
Then He put Adam into a deep sleep.

Then God took a rib from Adam,

And from it God made Eve,
He presented her to Adam,
Now to her alone he must cleave.

Adam said to God,
"She is bone from my bone,
And flesh of my flesh,
I am no longer alone."

Now the two of them were naked,
And they knew not any shame,
For they both were innocent,
And had no cause for blame.

They were very happy then,
As with God their time was spent,
But God's enemy the serpent,
Followed wherever they went.

He taunted Eve with these words;
"God lied about the knowledge tree."
He said, *"You would be very wise to listen to me."*

He told her that God lied about the fruit,
For it was good,
It would give them all God's knowledge,
As well as being tasty food.

So Eve gave into the temptation,
And picked the fruit to eat,
Then gave some of it to Adam,
Who was sitting at her feet.

Suddenly they knew the truth,

Of the terrible thing they had done,
How they had disobeyed their God,
And that the wicked devil had won.

Now all authority and dominion,
That God had given to man,
Was given into Satan's power,
And hindered God's perfect plan.

They were sent out of the garden,
And God covered them with skins,
Now they would have to work hard,
Regretting they had sinned.

And man would now need to be redeemed,
To be in fellowship with God once more,
But God in mercy had already planned,
For His Son to pay the price and fulfil the Law.

Taken From Genesis 3

ESTHER AND MORDECAI

There was a great King in the east,
Who made a feast one day,
He called for his Queen Vashti,
But she turned his servants away.

It made him very angry,
That she did not obey,
He said, *"I will have another Queen,
I'll start looking this very day."*

Now Mordecai the Jew,
Heard of this very thing,
So he took his niece Esther,
And presented her to the King.

The King thought she was beautiful,
But Mordecai knew,
That it would be better not to tell him,
That Esther was a Jew.

Some enemies in the land,
Plotted against the King,
When Mordecai heard of this,
The news to Esther he did bring.

But when Esther told the King,
She did not tell who it was that had saved him,
He didn't know it was the Jew,
So Haman the Agagite was promoted by the King.

All of the King's servants gave reverence to him,
Mordecai didn't, he bowed only to God,
To Haman he would not bow.
Said Haman when he heard of this,
"Mordecai is my enemy now."

He plotted to kill him,
With each and every Jew,
But of the Queen Esther,
Her lineage he never knew.

So he plotted to remove them all,
To banish them from this earth,
But to banish God's people,
Was more than his life was worth.

When Mordecai heard of his plan,
Once more to Esther he did go,
But what she could do about it,
At that time he did not know.

Queen Esther knew that she would die,
If the King would not accept her,
But when she came before him,
He held out his royal sceptre.

He then promised he would give her,
All that she would ask,

She asked him to come to a meal,
To enjoy a quiet repast.

She requested he bring Haman
To honour him too,
Then she would tell the King,
All that she wanted him to do.

All this was done by the Queen,
Because her uncle did insist,
That surely Esther had been born,
For such a time as this.

What Queen Esther did at the feast,
Soon everybody knew,
That the Queen had saved them,
By confessing she was a Jew.

So wicked Haman was caught out,
For the King now knew his plot,
The plan he had for Mordecai,
Was the one that Haman got.

Mordecai now knew,
The King was very happy with his wife,
They both took care of Mordecai,
For the rest of his life.

From the Old Testament book of Esther.

IN GOD'S SHADOW

When I dwell in the shadow of the Almighty,
Of a God who is faithful and just,
I will make Him my refuge and fortress,
For He is my God in whom I can trust.

He will deliver me from any plague,
From sickness and all of these things,
For He is my shield and buckler,
And I am very safe under His wings.

I have made the Lord my refuge,
And I will not fear the terror at night,
For God is guarding my dwelling,
With all of His power and might.

Many wars and battles may rage,
And thousands fall at my side I may see,
But I know I am safe from the battles,
For my God keeps them away from me.

Over me He gives His angels charge,
So my foot will not fall over a stone,
They will bear me up over them all,
For my God has not left me alone.

He has given me many promises,
That whenever evil I meet,
With His strength and love beside me,
I will trample it all under my feet.

For my God has set His love on me,
And I know that when I call on Him,
He will always set me free.

Taken from Psalm 91

ISAIAH'S COMMISSION

In the year that King Uzziah died,
Isaiah saw the Lord,
He also saw the Seraphim,
Who sang in one accord,
"Holy, Holy, Holy is the Lord."

The doors of the Temple opened,
The place was full of smoke,
Isaiah saw the Lord sitting on a throne,
Then in fear Isaiah spoke,

"Woe is me, woe is me," he cried,
*"My eyes have seen the King,
I am undone with unclean lips,
What repentance can I bring?"*

Then one of the Seraphim flew unto him,
Bearing a live coal in his hand,
Which he had taken from the fire with tongs,
Then Isaiah's lips he did brand,

"Now that this has touched your lips,"
He said, *"You are no longer in iniquity,
For all your sins are washed away,*

And clean your lips will be."

Then he heard the Lord's voice saying,
"Whom shall I send? Who will it be?"
Then Isaiah answering said,
"Here I am Lord, please send me."

Taken from Isaiah 6

JONAH

G od told Jonah to arise. He said,
   "I have a task for you to fill,
   I am sending you to Nineveh,
To tell them of my will.
Their sins are now so very bad,
I am calling them to repent."
But Jonah didn't want to go,
So to Nineveh he never went.

Instead he fled into a ship,
For to Tarshish he would go,
He hid in the ship's bottom,
Hoping that God would never know.
But God sent a storm to rock them,
And when the wind got worse,
The captain of the ship cried out,
"We are smitten with a curse."

They prayed for their gods to help them,
Then threw lots so they would know,
Who was to blame for the storm,
And why the stormy winds did blow.
When the lot fell on Jonah, they cried,
"Please call on your Lord."

"He is offended with me," Jonah said,
"You must throw me overboard."

So overboard they threw him,
Although this was not their wish,
Jonah sank into the sea,
And was swallowed by God's big fish.
This place he did not like at all
And after three whole days,
He was sorry and repented
And promised God to mend his ways.

Then God told the big fish,
To land Jonah on the beach,
Where he at once went to Nineveh,
And to the people began to preach.
He told them God was angry,
And of their sins they must repent,
If they did not, fire and brimstone,
To Nineveh would be sent.

They at once believed him,
And much to his dismay,
Putting on sackcloth and ashes,
They repented right away.
When God saw their repentance,
He was glad and said,
"I will not bring fire and brimstone pouring on their head."

This did not please Jonah,
He wanted brimstone to be poured,
So he sat in the sun and sulked,

When God in pity covered him with a gourd.
The sun soon dried the gourd up,
And beat once more on his head,
"Now even that is gone," he cried,
"I may as well be dead!"

This attitude of Jonah's really made God sad,
For although Nineveh was saved,
Jonah was not glad.
Let us not be like Jonah,
But be quick to obey the Lord,
For He is a forgiving God,
To all who believe His word.

Taken from the book of Jonah

THE PUBLICAN
OF JERICHO

Zacchaeus was a publican, much hated in Jericho,
When he heard of Jesus, he said,
"This man I'd like to know."
Zacchaeus was very small, in crowds he could not see.
"I know what I will do," he said,
"I will climb the sycamore tree."

From there his view was very good,
He could see all that Jesus did,
Up there he felt very safe,
For no one knew the place he hid.

But Jesus knew just where he was,
And when He passed by the tree,
He called to Zacchaeus saying,
*"I am coming to your house,
Prepare a meal for me."*

All the people cried out at this,
Surely this man was a sinner.
Was Jesus really going to his house,
To sit and eat His dinner?

Zacchaeus was touched in his heart,
And wanted to repent,
Of bad things he had done,
And the people's money he had spent.

He promised to repay it all,
To the people he had cheated.
He then told Jesus all of this,
When He and His friends were seated.

When Jesus heard all that Zacchaeus would do,
His heart filled with compassion, He said,
*"Salvation has come to this house,
For the old Zacchaeus is dead."*

From that day on, Zacchaeus lived a life so clean and true,
That all the people could see,
What great miracles Jesus could do.

Taken from Luke 19

BE LOVERS OF GOD

Be lovers of God dear children,
For He loves us with all of His might,
Walk in the love Jesus gave us,
Don't walk in the darkness, but light.

No stealing or unclean living,
No foolish talk, don't swear,
Do not covet your neighbour's goods,
His house, or what he does wear.

Be careful of those who lead you astray,
With trouble they are shod,
They want you to worship idols,
To turn you away from the one true God.

Be always filled with the Spirit,
Never turn away from the truth,
If doubt begins to fill your mind,
The Word of God is your living proof.

Make each and every day count,
Don't be foolish but be wise,
There is nothing worse in this world,
Than a man clever in his own eyes.

Be sure that all you do,
Can be shown in God's clear light,
For all things that are true,
Live in the day not the night.

Wives, submit to your husbands,
For they in Jesus, are head of their wives,
This will bring peace to your family,
For the rest of your lives.

Husbands, love your wives,
As Jesus loved the church He cherished,
For He plans to present her to God,
Without spot and without blemish.

Love your wife as you love yourself,
You care for your own flesh and bone,
You two are joined together for life,
And will never be on your own.

Give thanks always to God,
For all in Christ Jesus He has done,
For in Him was fought a great battle,
And in Him that battle was won.

So let us be filled with the Spirit,
Singing spiritual songs in one accord,
Giving our praise and worship,
To Christ Jesus our living Lord.

Taken from Ephesians 5

THE ARMOUR OF GOD

I will put on the 'Whole Armour of God,'
And be strong in His power and might.
I will stand against the wiles of the devil,
Wearing the Breastplate of Right.

We are not fighting this great battle,
Against beings of flesh and blood,
But against principalities so dark,
Trying to come in like a flood.

In God's army we are invincible,
And we are well able to stand,
With the Girdle of Truth about us,
And the Sword of the Spirit at hand.

Fiery darts of the wicked cannot harm us,
For we have God on our side,
In our hand we have the Shield of Faith,
Wearing Salvation's Helmet with pride.

We never run from the enemy,
With the Gospel of Peace we are shod,
We will fight until the very end,
For we are the Soldiers of God.

Taken from Ephesians 6

OPEN DOORS IN
THE BIBLE

I was meditating one day on how many times an open door was mentioned in my daily readings of the Bible.
It made me curious to find out more, and so here are some of my thoughts for you to read.
I hope that you will be blessed and encouraged to seek for more doors for yourself.

The first door that I found is in Exodus 12 v 22.

Here we have the instructions given to the Israelites by Moses, to take the blood of the lamb that they were told to prepare for their last meal in Egypt, and put it upon the lintel and door posts of their dwelling.

This was done in order that the Angel of Death would pass over them on his way to the Egyptians.

They were also told not to leave the house until morning. In other words not to go out into the dark.

In looking for a New Testament meaning for us today, I found that the blood on the lintel, which is above our heads and the blood on the door posts, that would be on either side of us, could portray the Blood of Jesus covering us and protecting on either side. Then I wondered why not on the doorstep?

Perhaps this could be showing us that, because Jesus died on the cross and defeated Satan, he was now under our feet.

The instruction not to leave the house in the hours of darkness, I saw as a good picture of our salvation in the 'new birth.'

We are saved from darkness and set free to live in the light, just as the Israelites were when they left their homes that morning.

The next door I found mentioned is in Exodus 21 v 5-6.

Here in these verses are God's instructions to a servant who wishes to stay with his master, even though he is freed.

He is brought before the judges and, his master takes him to a door post and pierces his ear with an aul (a type of needle.)

This was done to show everyone that, that servant had chosen to serve his master for the rest of his life.

What a wonderful picture of our choice to follow Jesus, our Master. For we choose to stay with Him when we come out of our slavery to Satan.

Our 'mark of slavery' which from then on is called 'bond slavery,' is the Holy Spirit living in us.

After this I moved on into the New Testament in John 10 v 7.

Jesus calls Himself 'the door of the sheep.'

He told the people this just before the parable of The Good Shepherd.

We, who have received Jesus as our Lord and Saviour have entered this door.

Praise God that Jesus is our shepherd.

I had a picture of goats entering in through Jesus (the door) and changing into 'sheep' on the other side.
The 'goats' in this picture of course are those who are not saved.

The next door I found mentioned is in Acts 14 v 27.
Here Barnabas and Paul are sharing with believers how God had opened 'the door of faith' to the Gentiles.
This obviously was a momentous thing to the Christian Jews.

1 Corinthians 16 v 9.
Here Paul witnesses at Ephesus that a great, effectual door had opened for him to preach.

2 Corinthians 2 v 12.
Paul tells us that a door was opened once again by God for him to be in Troas.
Here we learn that God is the door opener and that we should pray in all circumstances, that God will open doors for us too.

Colossians 4 v3.
Here Paul also prayed for God to open a door of utterance for himself and those with him.

James 5 v 9.
Here we are told not to hold anything against another, for the judge is standing at the door.
I wonder if this could be the door of Heaven?

Revelation 3.
Jesus tells the church at Philadelphia that He has set

before them an open door, that no man can shut.
This promise is also for us today for when the door of salvation is opened in our hearts, no one can close it.
As God's perfect will is that all should be saved, we should not neglect to tell people about Jesus every chance we get.

In Revelation 3 v 20, we see the most important door of all, with Jesus standing there knocking, waiting for us to open our hearts to invite Him in.

And so from Exodus to Revelation:-
Exodus 12 v 22 – *Door of Protection*.
Exodus 21 v 6 – *Door of Commitment*.
John 10 v 7 – *Door of Salvation*.
Acts 14 v 27 – *Door of Faith*.
1 Corinthians 16 v 9 – *Door of Effectiveness*.
2 Corinthians 2 v 12 – *Door of Witness*.
Colossians 4 v 3 – *Door of Utterance*.
James 5 v 9 – *Door of Judgement*.
Revelation 3 v 20 – *Door of Invitation*.

'Door' occurs in the Bible 189 times in 173 verses.
I have chosen just 10.

CHRISTIAN
RHYMES

MADE FOR GOD'S PLEASURE

When I read how God made me for His pleasure,
How He longs that I be made like His Son,
Shall I ever appreciate this treasure,
And praise Him all the day long?

Shall I live up to how much He loves me?
Will I ever love Him as much?
I know that Him, I long to see,
And by His Spirit feel His touch.

He has said I will l live up to His measure,
For He has promised to fulfil His work in me,
And I shall be one who gives Him pleasure,
For with His help, like His Son I shall be.

Now the things of this world have grown dim,
My Saviour means much more to me,
So I will leave the things of this world,
Yes I'll live in His light and be free.

COME LORD JESUS COME

There's a stirring up in Heaven,
A whispering in the wings,
"Is it time yet? Are we ready?
Has the Bridegroom got the rings?"

The angels that work in the stables,
Are putting all else aside,
They are grooming hordes of white horses,
For all of the saints to ride.

The warrior angels are busy too,
They are polishing shield and sword,
But these are only there for show,
For the battle is won by God's word.

The enemies of God start to tremble,
For they sense the stirring above,
But they still plan to battle,
Against the Son and His love.

I see Him standing before the throne,
He is there in full array,
He waits to hear His Father's word,
"Go my Son this is the day."

Then I woke up in my room,
Full of wonder of all I had seen,
A little saddened in my heart,
For it all had been a dream.

Then the wonder of that dream,
Began to dawn on me,
For the hope of every nation,
Was there for me to see.

So, Glory to God in the Highest,
And Praise to Lord Jesus His Son,
Let all of us shout together,
"Yes, Come Lord Jesus Come!"

THE FIRST EASTER

Jesus told His disciples to "Prepare the feast for today,
For I want to share it with you, before I go away.
You will see a man carrying water, in a pitcher on his head,
Follow him to his destination,
And enter where he has led.

There you are to prepare a room,
Make sure it is the upper,
For this is where we are going to eat,
What will be our last supper."

When they were gathered together,
Jesus told them that He would be betrayed,
By one who was eating with them,
It would be that very day.

The betrayer, he was Judas,
And before the feast would end,
Would have thirty pieces of silver,
In his hands to spend.

After supper they went into the garden,
Where Jesus went apart to pray,

For He knew the end was near,
The time for dying not far away.

He prayed, *"Father, if it be possible,*
Please take this task from me,
Yet not my will but yours be done,
For obedient I will be."

His disciples who had been asleep,
Woke, knowing something was amiss,
Then Judas appeared with many soldiers,
And betrayed Jesus with a kiss.

When the disciples saw this happen,
They were frightened and they fled,
For all the things that were happening,
Were just as Jesus had said.

The soldiers took Jesus to Pilate,
Who found no wrong in Him,
He wanted to release Him,
But the crowd made such a din.

For they had been persuaded to ask for Barabbas at the
feast,
They could have chosen Jesus for Pilate to release,
Then they flogged and mocked Him,
Putting a crown of thorns upon His head.

The disciples and those who loved Him,
Watched all of this with dread.
Then they hung Him on the cross,
"Father forgive them!" Jesus cried.
He committed His Spirit to God,

Bowed His head and died.

They buried Him in the garden tomb,
And sealed the door up tight,
They put some guards to watch the tomb,
All through the night.

Mary took many spices to visit the tomb next day,
But she saw with great amazement,
That the door was rolled away.
An angel of God was standing there,
In garments white as snow,
"Jesus has risen," he told her,
"To His disciples you must go."

She turned away to do this,
When the risen Jesus she did meet,
Her heart was filled with so much joy,
As she worshipped at His feet.

He told her, *"Do not be afraid,*
But do this task for me,
Go tell my disciples,
To meet me in Galilee."

The disciples did as Mary told them,
And there Jesus told them what to do,
"Go out into all the world," He said,
"And teach all that I taught you."

Then Jesus rose to Heaven,
And sat at God's right hand.
The disciples taught all that Jesus taught,
Helping people to understand,

That...

HE IS RISEN!!
HALLELUJAH!!!

A TALE AT CHRISTMAS

I'd like to tell you a Christmas story,
From a different angle somehow,
So I will tell you about a donkey,
A tiny mouse and a cow.

In days long ago these three friends,
Lived out their lives each day,
In a stable at the back of an inn,
So warmly filled with hay.

The owner of the donkey and cow,
Never knew about the mouse,
For the donkey and cow had warned him,
To be careful in the house.

The mouse was very clever,
And knew how to keep out of the way,
But he needed to look for food,
Because he couldn't eat the hay.

One night he was in the house,
Looking for crumbs on the floor,
When suddenly there was a knock,
Someone was at the door.

A man and a woman stood there,
They looked very weary to him,
Then he heard the master say,
"Sorry, we have no room at the Inn.

But you can stay in our stable,
If your baby is on the way,
In there it will be nice and warm,
With the animals and the hay."

The master who was really kind,
Gave them blankets wine and bread,
So the man took the woman to the stable,
And there made her a comfortable bed.

The mouse, the donkey and the cow,
Watched in wonder that night,
As the woman gave birth to a baby boy,
And the stable was filled with light.

And so the donkey, the mouse and the cow,
Watched over the baby in the manger,
Somehow they knew in their hearts,
This baby was no stranger.

I know this story began about the animals,
In a stable in days of old,
But would you believe it?
It's turned into the greatest story ever told.

For of course the man was Joseph,
And Mary was his wife,
And the baby, our Saviour Jesus,

Came to earth to give us new life.

So remember very clearly,
When you decorate your house,
About that wonderful night,
That blessed the donkey, the cow,
And of course, the tiny mouse.

MARWA'S MISSION

Marwa was from Africa,
A baptised Christian he became,
He changed his name from Marwa,
Now Emmanuel was his name.

He loved to hear the word of God,
At the meetings every week,
But no one gave him the answer to,
"What language does God speak?

When I get the answer" he said,
"My heart will fill with joy."
But no one had the answer,
For this inquisitive little boy.

The catechist said it was Latin,
Another said it was Greek,
None of these seemed right to him,
Still, there were other places to seek.

So he left his own dear country,
Although it was quite a wrench,
Across the world they told him,
God speaks Italian, English or French.

He went to the far land of China,
To be told God speaks Cantonese,
But Emmanuel knew in his heart,
That it was none of these.

Then he came to the land of God's people,
Believing they surely knew,
It still was not right when they told him,
God only speaks Hebrew.

By this time he was so weary,
And he needed a place to stay,
In Bethlehem they told him,
"Please go away."

Then in a cave he found a stable,
With a young mother and baby inside,
Mary said, *"Emmanuel you are welcome,
For you have travelled far and wide."*

He was amazed that she knew his name,
He wanted to ask how, but instead,
Somehow, he knew something good would happen,
If he listened to all Mary said.

*"You have travelled to find this one answer,
The language of God above,
I will tell you Emmanuel,
God's language is the language of love."*

Emmanuel knew in his heart of hearts,
This was the right answer at last,
The language of God was;

Love, for every nation and class.

For God loved the world so much,
That He gave His only Son,
So that all who believe in Him,
Would have eternal life, everyone.

ON THE MOUNT

When Jesus came upon the earth,
Many people gathered round,
Waiting to hear what He had to say,
They sat on rocks and on the ground.

As He stood on a hill above them,
He began to teach;
*"The Kingdom of God is near you,
It's no longer out of reach.*

The first commandment of value,"
He said, *"Comes from God above,
No other gods are you to serve,
Him only are you to love.*

*The second one also is true,
And this is the way to live,
To love your neighbour as yourself,
And always him forgive.*

*Don't let the poor go hungry,
Make sure he has a bed,
Supply him with the coat he needs,
Feed him with meat and bread.*

Don't let your heart go astray,
Or put your trust in leaven,
Don't store your treasure here on earth,
But store it all in Heaven."

Don't worry about anything,
About what you are to eat,
Don't think about what coat to wear,
Or what to put on your feet.

For God said 'Seek His Kingdom first,'
That is all you have to do,
Then all things that you may need,
Will be given unto you.

Don't think about tomorrow,
Of worries please beware,
Just put your trust in Father God,
And give Him every care.

If you seek Him you will find Him,
If you knock He will open the door,
If you ask it will be given you,
What loving Father could do more?"

They heard with joy all that Jesus said,
And would try to make it count,
They vowed to obey all that Jesus taught,
When He stood up on the mount.

BY HIS BLOOD

Use your divine imagination,
And picture Jesus' resurrection,
When He before His Father stood,
And offered up to Him His blood.

The blood that has the power,
To, on all who believe, shower,
The ability to go and share the light,
And fill creation with delight.

All who believe are cleansed from sin,
Pure white and holy, without and within,
Now we are sure of our Father's love,
And our future in the Kingdom above.

Now you can know the reality of this,
Not your imagination, but the pure bliss,
Of knowing God through Jesus' blood,
And being filled with His glorious love.

Come, use your imagination just once more,
And picture this in your mind's eye,
Our Lord and Saviour Jesus Christ,
Calling us up to meet Him in the sky.

DON'T FORGET

'm a believer in the Almighty God,
And I'd like to start a trend,
Where the Alpha and Omega would be,
The beginning and the end.

In every situation He would take a part,
In work, in sport, in music and every kind of art.
For He is the creator who made all things, and yet,
Those whom He created,
With closed hearts forget.

So open up your hearts and minds,
And open up closed ears,
Listen once more to your Father,
Whilst He takes away your fears.

Peace beyond understanding,
With love, is what you get,
When you open up your hearts and mind,
And Father God, you no longer forget.

FEAR NOT

"What is the world coming to?"
It's a cry we often hear,
Instead of enjoying our life,
We are living it in fear.

We and our children,
At home we often stay,
Because we feel it's dangerous,
To go out or to play.

For rapists and bombers,
Seem to want us hurt or dead,
It really is hard to understand,
What goes on in their head.

Many fought in the past,
A peace for us to win,
But to live in this peace it seems,
Depends on religion or the colour of your skin.

Here is a fact that artists know,
That stares us in the face,
That if you mixed the colours,
Of each and every race,

The colour you'd be left with,
Is the colour of the earth,
The colour of the dust,
From which God gave us birth.

How far away we have come,
From the teaching of our Lord,
Who taught that we should love and live in one accord.

So let us once more obey the law,
To love and to forgive,
Then we will live in peace once more,
And live and let others live.

For Christ Jesus came to teach all this,
If only we could hear.
We'd live our lives abundantly,
And not in strife or fear.

A RHYME FOR YOU

L ike a painter who looks at the world,
With brush strokes on his mind,
I find that nearly every thought,
Is not in prose but rhyme.

So if I wanted to tell you,
What God has done in my life,
How He healed me and set me free,
From every trouble and strife.

I would have to do it in rhyme,
That much now I do see,
So I always ask Christ Jesus,
To give a rhyme to me.

He has never left nor forsaken me,
His promises He'll always keep,
He is with me when I'm happy,
And with me when I weep.

And now I will tell you a wonder,
That all that Jesus has done for me,
If you ask Him, He will also do for you,
For He wants to set you free.

He will never leave nor forsake you,
He will be your friend through strife,
If you want to feel His healing touch,
You must ask Him into your life.

NO MATTER WHAT

If I were lost and deserted,
With all my loved ones gone,
My God would still be with me,
Sitting on my heart's throne.

And if that heart was breaking,
And my soul so full of grief,
My King would still be with me,
And His love would bring relief.

The world may say He's forgotten,
And that He does not care,
But I know that He loves me,
And He will always be there.

So Him I'll surely follow,
Until my earthly life ends,
And I will always be grateful,
For each blessing that He sends.

So join me now and praise Him,
For He loves us faithfully,
He sent His Son to die for us,
Yes He died for you and me.

FOUNTAIN OF LIFE

Your Word Lord is my life's fountain,
From which many times I drink,
Troubles like pits are before me,
I tremble there at the brink.

My poor heart nearly fails me,
But I know that I must be strong,
If it were not for Your Word's fountain,
My feelings and thoughts would be wrong.

I promised no trouble or pain would part us,
And oh! How those troubles have come,
All in my life is being tested.
Where would I be without Your Son?

For He is the Word and fountain,
From whence I can always drink,
He promised never to leave nor forsake me,
With His presence I will never sink.

So with that fountain's refreshing,
I will always be strong,
With Your help dear Father,
I'll keep going my whole life long.

PRAYER FOR TODAY

F ather we thank You,
For giving us Your Son,
For all that He will do for us,
And all that He has done.

He promises to answer,
If we humble ourselves and pray,
For all of the petitions,
We bring to You today.

We pray for the Queen,
And all her family,
That they will seek Your will Lord,
And be the rulers they should be.

We pray for the government,
That they will be filled,
With Your power and guidance,
To do the things You've willed.

We pray for our church Lord,
That we might be Your light,
That we may not be divided,
But in Your love unite.

We ask that you will help us,
In You to Holy be,
To keep us from temptation,
So from sin we will be free.

We praise and thank You Lord,
For what in Jesus name You will do,
And for the answers to the prayers Lord,
We have presented unto You.
Amen.

MY PRODIGAL SON

I loved my son so very much,
Gave him all that a mother could,
"You have spoilt him rotten." Friends would say,
Because like a boy, he wasn't always good.

What they never knew,
For they were never told,
Was that God would use him,
Before he was very old.

His ministry was music,
From God it was a gift,
Whenever we heard him play,
Our spirits would just lift.

But the enemy hated this,
And sent temptations very soon,
His so called friends led him astray,
And he started playing a different tune.

The road away from God was slippery,
And he fell into a slimy pit,
This brought him to his senses,
And he wanted to get out of it.

So, he turned away and paid the price,
For the crimes that he had done,
Turned right back to Father God,
And Jesus once more had won.

And now my dear son has gone away,
To stay with his Father God above,
Knowing that he is forgiven of all,
And safe in the arms of God's love.

REMEMBER...

R emember my dear,
When we sat in our special place,
The place where we met our Father,
To seek His face.

Remember the lovely birds,
That perched on railings in our view?
That fluttered, and then on tiny wings they flew.

Did they know dear heart,
That you were going to see the King,
That your spirit was about to fly away,
To hear the angels sing?

In welcome to such a faithful servant of the Lord,
Who had loved him with such care and kindness, All who
came to him.

On this earth dear one,
You are sorely missed by me your wife,
And all your family and friends,
But we will meet again when our time on this earth ends.

Then we too will hear the angels sing,
And be like you dear heart,

Safe in the arms of the King.

SHOW ME THE WAY

Show me the way oh Lord,
Tell me what to do,
Be the light unto my path,
For I want to follow you.

For I love You my Lord,
I love You my Lord.
In Your presence I always want to be,
I love You my Lord,
I love You my Lord,
I love You, 'cos You first loved me.

Now You have answered me,
And I know just what to do,
For You have led me to a well,
Where I can drink of You.

And I love You my Lord,
I love You my Lord,
In Your presence I will always be.

I love You my Lord,
I love You my Lord,
I love You 'cos You first loved me.

LITTLE LAUGHS

SENIOR MOMENTS

Just because we are OAP's,
It really doesn't mean,
That we have lost our faculties,
Or that our brains have left the scene.

I know that there are times,
When our minds can go quite blank,
But of course you know,
That it's a 'Senior Moment' you have to thank.

Forgetting someone's name too,
Can really be a bore,
But it's just a 'Senior Moment,'
It's really nothing more.

There you are chatting away,
Hoping they'll give you a clue,
But then you realise at last,
They've forgotten your name too.

I expect we'll always have them,
And I don't mind one or two,
'Cos if we didn't have them,
I couldn't write this rhyme for you.

AGE IS WHAT YOU FEEL

When there's a birthday to celebrate,
It makes me think about the days,
When I was only eighteen,
And very energetic in me ways.

But now my body has spread a bit,
With lumps all over the place,
And when I look in the mirror,
There are more lines upon me face.

My legs no longer want to run,
And my will to move is weak,
When I have been sitting long,
It's so hard to get to me feet.

The years fly faster and faster,
And the weeks are gone in a flash,
The world is so much different now,
And seems to be heading for a crash.

Although all these signs seem very bad,
There is something I have to say,
Inside, the years are put on hold,
And eighteen I'll always stay.

So let's not think about our age,
And about the times to come,
Because if you only feel eighteen,
Life can be a lot of fun.

ANTS AND THINGS

When does an ant have a holiday?
I'd really like to know,
Cause that's when I'd have a picnic,
With goodies all on show.

It really is annoying,
When I've bit into my bread,
To see this wriggling black thing,
Before my eyes, minus head.

They ought to go on a package deal,
With wasps and creepy things,
And all the other creatures,
With multiple legs and stings.

I know where I'd like to send them,
A big grin on my face,
I'd pack them all in a rocket,
And send them to outer space.

To all of God's creatures,
I try to be very good,
But I really do find it hard,
To like them in my food.

It beats me how such little things,
Can put us on the run,
To have them buzzing round you,
Really is not fun.

So I'm putting up a petition,
To send them all away,
Then we can enjoy our picnic,
On this lovely sunny day.

ANOTHER DAY

When I wake up in the morning,
I try hard to say,
"Thank you Lord so very much,
For giving me another day."

Although my body does creak and moan,
When I first open up my eyes,
That I am still alive,
Quite fills me with surprise.

I don't exactly jump out of bed,
I have to take it slow,
And wait for all the kinks,
In my creaky body to go.

But then when I am up,
And put the kettle on,
I make myself a cup of tea,
And all the kinks are gone.

I switch on the news on the tele,
I like to watch News 24,
Then when I hear of all the trouble in the world,
I can't think of mine anymore.

Instead I ask the Lord,
What can I do to make a change,
"Just love the people around you," He said,
"And pray always for those out of range."

This advice I want to follow,
And hope that I can make a change,
And love all those around me,
Praying for those out of range.

IMAGINATION

H ave you ever stared at a pattern,
On wallpaper or carpeted floor,
At first you see the pattern,
And then you see much more.

The flowers become faces,
With waving leaves of hair,
Then as you go on staring,
Many more pictures appear.

I can see dancing fairies and elves,
On my net curtain on the window,
Then when I blink my eyes,
They're gone, I wonder where they go.

The carpet now is wonderful,
As I gaze in imagination,
Why look! There is a steam engine,
Puffing at the station.

And surely that's a dragon,
Breathing fire on that mountain,
And isn't that an elephant,
Drinking water at a fountain?

Of course this could go on,
For as long as I want to stare,
Would you believe it, that dragon,
Has turned into a snarling bear.

Now things are getting lively,
As animals chase around the floor,
Oh dear, I have to stop now,
Because there's someone at the door.

As I told my friend, what I had been doing,
She threw a very strange look at me,
And said, *"I think you better sit down,*
While I make you a nice cup of tea."

Now I wonder, why did she say that?

NOW LET ME THINK

As I gaze into my wardrobe,
With many ideas I do flirt,
Now shall I wear my trousers,
Or be daring in a skirt?

I'm stood before the mirror,
My mind so full of doubt,
Shall I tuck my jumper in,
Or shall I leave it out?

Having made my mind up,
Did I hear you say, 'Hurray!'
I know that you are thinking,
'Does she have to take all day?'

Now that I have finished,
It's time to don my coat,
But looking out of the window,
It's raining, that's really got my goat.

So I'll have to change my mind again,
That really is a bind,
Instead of putting on my coat,
It's my mac I have to find.

You may think all this is trivial,
That it really doesn't matter,
But if you have a body such as mine,
Dreams of fashion soon will shatter.

So I will gaze into my wardrobe,
And with ideas I will flirt,
I'll make up my mind to wear trousers,
Then I'll change into a skirt.

TEN MINUTES IN THE BATHROOM

Ten minutes in the bathroom,
Is all it takes these days,
To happily face the world outside,
With a smile upon me face.

Sitting in the bathroom,
Gazing at the tiles,
Listening to the fizzing,
Of Steradent round me smile.

As I patiently sit there waiting,
I look back upon the scene,
When a quick go with a toothbrush,
Got me smile nice and clean.

But sadly those days are over,
And the days of fixative are in,
And as I sit here in the bathroom,
You wouldn't like me toothless grin.

Now I'll tell you a secret,
That I've never told before,
Nobody has seen me without me smile,

'Cos I shut the bathroom door.

Of course that isn't quite true,
There is one who's seen that toothless grin,
Yes that's right, you've guessed it,
It's the dentist who put them in.

Well now the waiting is over,
And under the tap me smile does go,
So I am ready to share these thoughts with you,
And put on a big smile before I go.

THE THINGS WE SAY

If we took some things as literal,
I wonder what it would be like,
To find yourself quickly pedalling,
When told to, *"Get on your bike!"*

And if it really rained 'cats and dogs'
What panic you would meet,
With poodles, Siamese and such,
Falling all over the street.

But wouldn't it be fun,
If when dining with a friend,
They said, *"Get away with you!"*
And you landed in Southend.

What if I were so very light,
That you could 'knock me down with a feather,'
I really would have to watch it,
If I was out in windy weather.

Of course we'd know it was not true,
If we heard some people scoff,
That joke was really funny for,
'I nearly laughed my head off.'

The picture this brings to mind,
I would not like to see,
For sometimes I can be funny,
And you would put the blame on me.

I remember in times way back,
That my mother used to say,
"I've got eyes in the back of my head,
So don't try to sneak away!"

This really used to scare me,
Though I said that I didn't care,
But I couldn't help looking,
For those eyes, peeping through her hair.

I have enjoyed writing this,
And I wonder what you think,
For now I've got it 'off my chest,'
I am really 'in the pink.'

I know there must be many more,
Funny things that people say,
If you can think of any more,
I'd like to hear them all one day.

EPILOGUE

TO SHOW THE WAY

Jesus gave us a commission,
To tell of His Kingdom above,
And to show to as many as possible,
The wonder of His love.

He has not left us quite alone,
To fulfil this, not so easy task,
But promises always to be with us,
To give help whenever we ask.

He has shown us in His Word,
The way that we must go,
To follow Him in everything,
Is really the way you know.

I want to share with you,
That Jesus has you on His heart,
Of all His joy and happiness,
He wants you to have a part.

So if you have a burden,
That you would like to share,
We, who love the Lord, will listen,
For we want to show you that we care.

There was a time, when Jesus I did not know,
And I had many a burden to bear,
But then someone who knew Jesus,
Showed me that the Lord God cares.

They prayed for me to know Him,
And He answered right away,
Suddenly the world was brighter,
It was like turning night into day.

And now each time I have a problem,
I look to my God above,
And He always gives me the answer,
For He is the God of love.

So do not let the devil abuse you,
By giving you troubles and strife,
For God gave you His Son Jesus,
To give you abundant life.

And I know it does not matter,
If now your hair is white,
For to Father God, you're just a child,
That He wants to hug real tight.

A MESSAGE FROM TRISH

I do pray that you have been blessed by reading my book and that you will seek Jesus for yourself if you don't already know Him.

'For God so loved the world that He gave His only Son, that all may have eternal life.' (John 3v16)

The sins of the whole world have been forgiven because Jesus paid the price for them all on the cross.
All we have to do is believe and receive this free gift of Salvation.

This is all I had to do to be born again and filled with the Holy Spirit.
God did not point my sins out to me, but when I received His love, I knew I was a sinner but I had been washed clean and was free to have fellowship with Father God for eternity.

I pray this for you too dear reader.

God bless you.

BOOKS BY THIS AUTHOR

The Gospel Of Matthew In Rhyme

The Bible has most of it's poetry in the Hebrew of the Old Testament.

There are the 'Poetic Books' of Job, Psalms, Proverbs, Song of Songs, Ecclesiastes and Lamentations.

There are also great sections of poetry in the prophetic books, such as Isaiah.

Anything that helps us read God's word today is to be encouraged.

In this book, Trish has wonderfully put together the Gospel of Matthew into poetic form.

Printed in Great Britain
by Amazon

58279150R00058